To: Mom

♡: Nikki

I love You

2010

Simple Truths of Life

A COLLECTION OF LESSONS LEARNED

To the friends and family who have laughed and cried
over my poems and stories throughout the years.
Your laughter and your tears are a part of me
and a part of my writings.
Your encouragement has inspired me to inspire others.
Therefore, I dedicate this book to each of you …
with gratitude and love.
~ Linda

Published by Simple Truths
1952 McDowell Road, Suite 205
Naperville, IL 60563-65044

Design: Rich Nickel

Photos:
Cover: Veer
Shutterstock page 7,
istockphoto, pages 10, 17, 21, 24, 28, 33, 37, 38, 43, 47, 50, 55, 59, 63, 66, 70, 72,
76, 80, 85, 88, 93, 94, 98, 108, 113, 117, 120, 125,132, all background textures
Fotolia page 102
Todd Reed Photography : www.toddandbradreed.com page 144

Printed and bound in the United States of America

ISBN 978-1-60810-058-3

01 WOZ 09

Contents

There is an unspoken balance
that time has clearly explained
between what I've lost over the years
and all that I have gained ...

Every trait that I surrender
as I slowly "lose" my youth
is replaced with a life's lesson;
traded for ...
a Simple Truth.

I am the product of my years;
they have created what is me.
And every day that I have lived
has made me who I want to be.

Each person I have known or loved
is a part of who I am today.
Each left me something in my life;
each helped me find my way.

I've heard it said, "If I knew then
everything that I know now ..."
But we are taught at the proven pace
that time ... and life ... will both allow.

These truths I've learned
from things I've done
and places I have been ...
what I'd give to take them back with me
and live my life again.

I've learned it is much easier

to speak only what is true

because lies are just like boomerangs; they will soon come back to you.

A Simple Truth About ...

Honesty

7

People grow through experience if they
meet life honestly and courageously.
This is how character is built.

ELEANOR ROOSEVELT

One of the most striking differences
between a cat and a lie
is that a cat has only nine lives.

MARK TWAIN

He who tells a lie is not sensible of
how great a task he undertakes; for he must be forced
to invent twenty more to maintain that one.

ALEXANDER POPE

There is no twilight zone of honesty …
A thing is right or it's wrong. It's black or it's white.

John F. Dodge

A single lie destroys a whole reputation for integrity.

Baltasar Gracian

Honesty is the first chapter in the book of wisdom.

Thomas Jefferson

A Simple Truth About ...

People

I've learned to eliminate indifference
and the cold effect of nonchalance;
now whenever I ask, "How are you?"
I'll stick around for a response.

One Lucile

Recently experiencing the metamorphosis of my beloved hobby, creative writing, becoming a business involving contracts and lawyers, I have become convinced that the only way the human race survives, and continues to thrive despite itself, is due to an unspoken and delicate balance. I am referring to my own version of the well-known balance between good and evil, calibrated on a more human scale, which I have dubbed the balance between the unscrupulous and the Luciles.

I've even gone so far as to develop a "Lucile equation" in my mind. It helps me to mentally cope with those inevitable and unavoidable encounters with those folks who, through their own actions of chicanery, make me question my own compassion, understanding and patience. As an inspirational writer in this world, some days it's difficult to be truly inspired. I often feel like, in a line borrowed from the show *Cheers,* "It's a dog eat dog world and I'm wearing Milk Bone underwear." Yet, I've found that there are still many of us who maintain belief in a "good will overcome evil" philosophy.

Though increasingly more cautious, we tend to remain naive and unsuspecting of the unscrupulous who, like hungry lions, hide in the shadows waiting for opportunities to pounce.

Using what my family affectionately calls "Linda Logic," I've created the following equation: For every ten unethical, immoral or dishonest people, there is One Lucile to maintain the balance…

Recently, on a dreary, rainy day with one of my routine sinus headaches slowly rearing its ugly head, I stopped at a well-known hamburger chain. (Though I've made respectable strides toward rehabilitation, I am admittedly a junk food junkie and that day, I needed a fix!)

When I placed my tray on the table, I felt a cool chill from the vent positioned directly above my seat, so I quickly relocated to another table. An elderly woman, one row over, facing my newly chosen location, happened to notice my shiver and said to me with animated motions, "There's a vent over here, too. It's chilly in here!"

I smiled back at her and nodded in complete agreement. Apparently this friendly acknowledgement was, to her, an invitation to begin one of the most enlightening and enjoyable conversations I can remember having in many years.

It began with talk about our recent rainfall deficit and soon blossomed into stories of her children, her recently installed pacemaker, President Truman, and her personal opinions on rising gas prices and those who oppose drilling for oil in the U.S.

I quickly noted that she was very intelligent. During the next 45 minutes, I eagerly learned of her children, her strong belief in God and the fact that she'd survived cancer at the age of 38. One of her most memorable statements was when she said, "I told each of my children that they do not belong to me. They belong to God and he loaned them to me to do the best that I can." Another statement referred to the news she'd received almost 50 years prior, that she had cancer. She said she prayed to God to give her just enough time to raise her children. Then she added humbly, "And look how much more He's given me. I'm 87 years old and the first thing I do every morning is thank Him for yet another day."

In her stories, she referenced her husband, but didn't share how he'd passed. Though she still proudly donned a gold wedding band, I surmised that he must be deceased because all of her statements used the "I" pronoun, never "we." My "angel of the day" said things to me that afternoon that I won't forget. At one point, she looked at me sincerely and said, "God bless you and enjoy your life, honey. It goes by so fast."

When it was time for our unexpected "visit" to end, she stood up with her tray, faced the front counter staff and with a charming exuberance exclaimed, "Thank you! That was DELICIOUS!" With that, I smiled and followed her out the door.

In 2005, my first gift book was published, co-authored by Mac Anderson, and titled *"The Dash…Making a Difference with Your Life."* It is a book about how you spend your dash, that little line on your tombstone between the dates of birth and death.

I happened to have an extra copy in my car and offered it to Lucile as a gift because it reflected the perceptions of life she'd chosen to share with me that rainy afternoon. Well, you'd have thought I'd offered her the moon. She clutched it to her chest with both hands and said she'd cherish it forever. I offered to sign it for her and before I'd completed the sentence, she leaned forward to see what I was writing, tapped her finger on the page and replied excitedly, "That's Lucile…with one "L!"

I thanked her for her wisdoms, wished her well and walked to my car. As I started the engine, I heard a horn beep twice. I turned to see her driving away and blowing a kiss in my direction.

I left that day with a renewed outlook. It felt, in a way, as though my heart was smiling.

First Impressions

I've learned not to rely on first impressions
for things aren't always as they seem.
Sometimes the very smallest player
is the best one on the team.

17

I've never met a person, I don't care what his
condition, in whom I could not see possibilities.

PRESTON BRADLEY

Be not swept off your feet by the vividness of the
impression, but say, "Impression, wait for me
a little. Let me see what you are and
what you represent. Let me try you."

EPICTETUS

To avoid assumptions, ask questions.
It takes courage to trust the present moment,
to allow other people to be exactly who they are,
and to let life unfold according to its own plan…
and it avoids a great deal of suffering.

DON MIGUEL RUIZ

Beware, as long as you live,
of judging people by appearances.

JEAN DE LA FONTAINE

The worst mistake of first contact, made throughout
history by individuals on both sides of every new
encounter, has been the unfortunate habit of making
assumptions. It often proved fatal.

DAVID BRIN

Begin challenging your own assumptions.
Your assumptions are your windows on the world.
Scrub them off every once in a while,
or the light won't come in.

ALAN ALDA

19

A Simple Truth About ...

Anger

I've learned that words are permanent;
hearts cannot be unbroken
and saying "I'm sorry" cannot retrieve
angry words that I have spoken.

Make What's Left, Right

When we are young, we never really consider that we will eventually grow old. We know it's a fact, yet the true reality doesn't sink in until much later. When you are 17, thinking of yourself as an 85-year-old doesn't even seem fathomable. Even as we grow older and reach milestones such as 30, 40 and beyond, we don't realize that the number of years behind us is silently, and with rapidly increasing momentum, catching up with, and inevitably surpassing, the years we anticipate are in front of us. This epiphany didn't hit me until I was celebrating the "third anniversary" of my 40th birthday.

So, of course, I started to make some changes around that time. Not that I had been living my life as a shrew, but I felt I could definitely use some positive changes, especially when it occurred to me that I hadn't a clue how much time was in front of me. In my mind, I pictured my lifeline as a see-saw with one side representing the years that had passed and the other side, those remaining. (The heavy kid was sitting on the side of my past!)

Being unaware of our remaining time is a good thing. For instance, if at some point, we knew that we had a definite 40 years in front of us, some of us might choose to live in sin and depravity for 39 years and 11 months and then make restitution around mid-December of month 12. It reminds me of "sweeps week" with network television; that period in which viewing figures are calculated for various shows and channels. During these times, networks deliberately bring out new episodes, series and specials in an effort to boost their viewing figures, and therefore, advertising revenue.

However, the mere notion that we don't know if we have 40 years, 40 minutes or 40 seconds is the basis for the title of this story, *Make What's Left, Right*. None of us are guaranteed a tomorrow. Whether you are 19 or 91 reading this story today, you could have the same amount of time remaining on this earth and the same amount of time to take the necessary steps to make what's left, right. The positive changes you've been thinking about making "someday" or those fences you've been meaning to mend need to be done now. **Don't put off making worthwhile changes because you expect or anticipate that you have a certain amount of time.** This type of procrastination could end with a "too little, too late" result.

Money

I've learned that possessions
do not determine your wealth
and that plastic credit cards
are "debtrimental" to your health.

More people should learn to tell their dollars
where to go instead of asking them
where they went.

ROGER W. BABSON

The real measure of our wealth is how much
we should be worth if we lost our money.

J.H. JOWETT

The holy passion of friendship is so sweet
and steady and loyal and enduring in nature
that it will last through a whole lifetime,
if not asked to lend money.

MARK TWAIN

Money often costs too much.

RALPH WALDO EMERSON

Wealth consists not in having great
possessions, but in having few wants.

EPICTETUS

Some debts are fun when you are
acquiring them, but none are fun when you
set about retiring them.

OGDEN NASH

A Simple Truth About ...

Cautiousness

I've learned though we try to shield our children
from life's hardships and life's pain ...
there will always be occasions in life
when a kid needs to walk in the rain.

The surest way to make it hard for children
is to make it easy for them.

ELEANOR ROOSEVELT

One way you can often do more
for your child is to do less.

ENGLISH PROVERB

You cannot teach a child to take care of himself
unless you will let him try to take care of himself.
He will make mistakes; and out of these mistakes
will come his wisdom.

HENRY WARD BEECHER

Do not handicap your children by
making their lives easier.

ROBERT A. HEINLEIN

At every step the child should be allowed to
meet the real experiences of life;
the thorns should never be plucked from the roses.

ELLEN KEY

We want our children to grow up to be such persons
that ill-fortune, if they meet with it,
will bring out strength in them,
and that good fortune will not trip them up,
but make them winners.

EDWARD SANDFORD MARTIN

A Simple Truth About ...

Moments

I've learned to differentiate
each moment from each minute:
A minute is but a measure of time,
but a moment is what's in it.

It is life's moments that define the years
and chronicle our past …
mile markers of a journey
that is over much too fast.

LINDA ELLIS

Moments … those precious blocks of time preserved in

our minds as virtual photos. Our memories are completely made up of life's
moments. It is those particular, unique moments in life — the good and the
bad, that will be remembered and repeatedly recalled from the archives of
our memories as the years roll on. The year, time and date of a moment's
occurrence only prove to be insignificant data, which fades over time, but
the recollection of a moment itself can be crystal clear.

The word moment is described by Webster as "a comparatively brief period of time." Not a minute … not an hour … but a moment; a specific point
in time that is not measurable by seconds, minutes or hours. It is as
though the mind has its own database where the notable, quotable hap-
penings are stored away as our journey progresses. Then something hap-

pens and a moment from the past that's been filed away and temporarily forgotten is again brought to the forefront to be relived and retold.

I can, without hesitation, recall the first time I felt the gentle movement of my baby's first "kick" inside. I can picture with complete clarity her first smile and the first time she laughed aloud, but I cannot remember the precise date or time. I can picture the scene when I caught my first fish and the proud expression on my father's face, but I have no idea what month or year it was. And when life is offering nothing but stressful moments, I can, at will, escape to those moments in my mind when I was walking barefoot slowly along the ocean's shore. I can almost feel the warm sand between my toes and hear the steady roar of the continuous crashing waves. I close my eyes and imagine the sensation of breathing the fresh, salt-water air into my lungs. Such details are preserved and contained in our minds only within the moments we have lived and experienced. I am able to relive these moments so vividly, not because I saw them on television or experienced them through the "virtual reality" that is the Internet, but because I was there. They are unique to my life, my past and all that is me, and they are mine to cherish forever.

"Occasionally in life there are those

moments of unutterable fulfillment

which cannot be completely explained

by those symbols called words.

Their meanings can only be articulated

by the inaudible language

of the heart."

MARTIN LUTHER KING, JR.

A Simple Truth About ...

Loss

I've learned that when you lose someone
who is a part of who you are ...
time will surely heal the wound,
but it won't erase the scar.

Your absence has gone through me
Like thread through a needle.
Everything I do is stitched with its color.

W.S. MERWIN

In times of deep sorrow it is not the people who tell you why
you are suffering who are of any use; the people who help
you are those who give expression to your state of mind;
often they do not speak at all.

OSWALD CHAMBERS

Sad soul, take comfort, nor forget
the sunrise never failed us yet.

CELIA THAXTER

In this sad world of ours,

sorrow comes to all,

and it often comes with bitter agony.

Perfect relief is not possible,

except with time.

You cannot now believe that you will ever feel better.

But this is not true.

You are sure to be happy again.

Knowing this, truly believing it,

will make you less miserable now.

ABRAHAM LINCOLN

Education

I've learned that basic common sense,
the foundation of true "knowledge,"
is gained more from living life each day
than from courses at a college.

43

It is a thousand times better to have common sense
without education than to have education
without common sense.

ROBERT G. INGERSOLL

Common sense ain't common.

WILL ROGERS

The great end of education is to discipline
rather than to furnish the mind; to train it to the use
of its own powers, rather than fill it with the
accumulation of others.

TRYON EDWARDS

Earth and sky, woods and fields, lakes and rivers,
the mountain and the sea, are excellent schoolmasters,
and teach some of us more than we can
ever learn from books.

JOHN LUBBOCK

The things we know best are the things
we haven't been taught.

MARQUIS DE VAUVENARGUES

No one tests the depth of a river with both feet.

ASHANTI PROVERB

A Simple Truth About ...

Optimism

I've learned that remaining positive
is the most effective way to cope
because there's really not much left to give
once you've given up on hope.

Dash of Hope

My poem, *"The Dash"* was the subject of a gift book, co-authored by Mac Anderson. The poem is based on that little line on a tombstone, between the dates of birth and death. Ultimately, that dash is a symbol which represents every day we've spent alive on earth. Therefore, how you spend your "dash" is all that really matters. Following is an amazing story about someone whose dash truly made a difference...

Recently I heard about a little girl named Hope Stout. After learning more about her life, I couldn't help but feel it was not by coincidence, nor happenstance, that she had been named "Hope." It had to be attributed to fate. The compassion and generosity housed in her young heart made a lasting impression on me and countless others, and her legacy of love continues to bless lives every day. Though I never had the opportunity to meet her, I wish I had. It seems as though she was wise beyond her tender years and very, very special. When I tell people her story, I always say, "if this doesn't inspire you, I don't think there's much that could ..."

Hope was a twelve-year-old girl who was offered a "wish" in early December 2003 by the "Make-A-Wish" Foundation after being informed that she had a rare type of bone cancer. However, when she found out that more than 150 children in her area were waiting for their wishes to be granted, she unselfishly used her wish to ask that those children have their wishes granted. She also asked that it be done by January 16, 2004. Unfortunately, however, the organization informed her that her noble request could not be granted as the funds were simply unavailable. They calculated that they would need to raise more than one million dollars in thirty days in order to grant her wish. Disappointed, but not discouraged, she turned her dismay into an enthusiasm that inspired caring individuals to spearhead fundraising to help grant the wishes of the other children, and eventually hers as well. Newspaper columnists and reporters for radio and TV stations shared the story of this caring young girl who had touched the hearts of so many and as word spread, the community was challenged. Committees were formed and schools, corporations and various organizations assisted in raising money to help bring Hope's dream to fruition.

Though she lost her battle in 2004, knowing that her wish was going to come true, Hope lives on. Her heartfelt efforts were not in vain as they continue to help others, not only physically, but spiritually and emotionally as well. At the initial fundraiser and gathering to celebrate her life, "A Celebration of Hope" on January 16, 2004, the announcement was made that they had indeed received donations totaling more than one million dollars on behalf of Hope Stout. **Her wish had been granted!**

DETOUR
AHEAD

A Simple Truth About ...

Disappointment

I've learned that it's easier to cope
with closure or rejection
when you recognize each as a simple detour
guiding you in a new direction.

Our real blessings often appear to us in the shape
of pains, losses and disappointments.

Joseph Addison

The size of your success is measured by the
strength of your desire; the size of your dream; and
how you handle disappointment along the way.

Robert Kiyosaki

Disappointment to a noble soul is what cold water
is to burning metal; it strengthens, tempers,
intensifies, but never destroys it.

Eliza Tabor

If we will be quiet and ready enough, we shall find compensation in every disappointment.

HENRY DAVID THOREAU

Was yesterday a disappointment? I am sorry. But this is another day. The earth has turned around since yesterday. Face the New Day with good cheer!

HENRY F. HENRICHS

Disappointment is often the salt of life.

THEODORE W. PARKER

A Simple Truth About ...

Growing Up

I've learned that maturity comes only from many years of give and take ... not from the total number of candles on your last birthday cake.

Maturity begins to grow when you can
sense your concern for others outweighing
your concern for yourself.

JOHN MACNAUGHTON

If we don't change, we don't grow.
If we don't grow, we are not really living.
Growth demands a temporary surrender of security.

GAIL SHEEHY

To make mistakes is human;
to stumble is commonplace;
to be able to laugh at yourself is maturity.

WILLIAM ARTHUR WARD

Life is change. Growth is optional. Choose wisely.

KAREN KAISER CLARK

Maturity is the time of life when, if you had the time,
you'd have the time of your life.

UNKNOWN

Maturity is:
The ability to stick with a job until it's finished;
The ability to do a job without being supervised;
The ability to carry money without spending it; and
The ability to bear an injustice without
wanting to get even.

ABIGAIL VAN BUREN

A Simple Truth About ...

Stress

I've learned it is okay to answer "no"

with strong tenacity

for even a large, porous sponge

reaches its capacity!

There's a quote I bought on a framed print that reads:

"Life is hard, yard by yard. Inch by inch, it's a cinch."

Stress

My brother John, better known within the family as a "creative genius," had his own version of this perception. He once told me, during one of the more harried periods of his life, that he'd like to take his brain out and rinse it. At first I laughed, but as the years have passed, I've often wished, theoretically at least, that I could do that very thing … just rinse off the "clutter" and the unnecessary thoughts that continually bog down my mind and prevent me from living in the moment and being able to just "be."

In this busy time, we often have trouble concentrating on the task at hand. I remember one day about ten years ago when I came in after grocery shopping with my two little girls. I had my arms full of bags and literally dropped them on the floor as I closed the door behind me. Both girls ran quickly in opposite directions to avoid being asked to help put the groceries away.

I was busy putting everything in its place when I heard a knock on the door. I looked out the peephole and saw a man standing there with a clipboard. I was annoyed, to be honest, because that's the last thing I needed! I peered out the window in a disapproving manner and made a visual sign (much like an umpire's "out") that we were not interested. I turned to walk away when I heard knock, knock, knock. I thought to myself, great … just great … all I need is a persistent salesman tonight. I went back to the window, opened it this time and told him I was not interested in whatever he was peddling. There! With that, I closed and locked the window.

I turned to walk away and again heard knock, knock, knock. This time I got nervous, so I brought my man-eating golden retriever,
who would no doubt lick this would-be intruder's face, before showing him where my jewelry was kept. I opened the window another six inches and again repeated that I was not interested. To which this gentleman politely replied, *as he held my dangling key ring in front of the window,* "I thought you might need these …"

Apparently, in my haste, I left the house keys hanging from the front door lock.

I quickly replied to the young man, "Oh … uhm … thanks. What were you selling? I'll buy twelve…"

Marriage

I've learned a good marriage is like a brick wall
that withstands any weather
and love is simply the mortar
that holds it all together.

Story writers say that love is concerned only
with young people, and the excitement and
glamour of romance end at the altar.
How blind they are. The best romance is inside
marriage; the finest love stories come after
the wedding, not before.

IRVING STONE

May there be such a oneness between you in
your marriage that when one of you weeps,
the other will taste salt.

MARTIN BUXBAUM

Chains do not hold a marriage together.
It is threads, hundreds of tiny threads, which sew
people together through the years.

SIMONE SIGNORET

The marriages we regard as the happiest are those
in which each of the partners believes that
he or she got the best of it.

SYDNEY J. HARRIS

A Simple Truth About ...

Emotions

I've learned that sorrow and happiness
have a fine line between either,
but with tears, as well as laughter,
it is best to hold back neither.

Popsicles

As the caregivers for my father during the weeks preceding his imminent demise, my brother Bill and I, having a reputation within the family as care-free, silly and bordering on nonsensical when paired together, were faced with the harsh reality of reality.

Day after day we watched as the cancer did what it does best: taking a life and breaking the hearts of those who held that life dear. We offered him anything, everything we could imagine, be it useful or inane. We would have done anything for him during that painful time…yet we were reduced to fulfilling his requests for half glasses of water, pillows, the remote control and the telephone. He couldn't eat food in any form, solid or puréed. He couldn't drink anything of substance, small sips of water. Our hearts ached to help him in some way…large or small. I remember at one point, looking at my father and saying in anguish, "I wish there was something I could DO to help." He replied, "You're doing it, sweetheart, you're doing it." I assumed at the time he meant my presence there (as functionally useless as it may have been) was making a difference and that reassured me.

Breaking the monotones of an almost silent room, a *Star Trek* episode played on TV as my father pretended to watch it intently in an effort to curtail our repeated suggestions as to his possible wants or needs. The irony struck me as my subconscious slowly absorbed Captain Picard's words in the background… *Our options are limited…there must be a way…*

I faintly remember the inflections in the voice of a hopeful man, not yet defeated, but well on his way. In hindsight, it's as though my life was running parallel to that of this fictitious character, as we were struggling simultaneously with an issue whose positive resolution seemed unattainable. And as he quickly arose from his Captain's chair on the bridge with renewed determination, my father turned his focus away from the TV, and in his weakened voice said, "Maybe popsicles. I might be able to eat a popsicle." A request! Although small and somewhat insignificant in hindsight, it was still a request!

My brother and I looked at each other. Our eyes widened with excitement! Popsicles! Pop wants popsicles! Looking back, we were unusually overjoyed at the concept, and in our haste to get out the door I think we bumped into each other three times. The recollection of the event brings to mind an episode of *The Keystone Cops.* I grabbed the keys, forgot my purse and accidentally put on my brother's shoes. We were going to the store to buy popsicles! Something—albeit so trivial in the grand scheme of the situation—here at last was something we could do to ease his pain, maybe subtract from his discomfort, if only for just a little while. No, this wasn't going to cure his cancer. No, this wasn't going to take away his pain. But, as helpless as we were beginning to feel, it was indeed *something* we could do.

With that, we raced to the car, solemn and completely focused on our mission. As soon as we arrived at the grocery store, we grabbed a cart and our quest began. Our subconscious intent was to purchase every popsicle brand and flavor known to man as we proceeded to search for the popsicle

 section. Racing through the store as if these magic popsicles were somehow going to save the day, and placing our own imaginary urgency upon this task, our eyes scoured the aisles…ice cream…frozen pies…fudge pops…WHERE DOES THIS DARN STORE KEEP THE POPSICLES? We frantically searched the rows, as if we were participants in a scavenger hunt competing for the main prize of a new Cadillac. Suddenly we looked up at the sign: "Frozen Desserts" and I remember feeling as though I'd seen an American Flag gracefully blowing in the breeze after trying to flee from a third-world country. We immediately positioned our imaginary borders and examined the sections under our command, he on one end of the frozen dessert aisle, and I on the other. Then, I heard his voice proclaim, "I FOUND THEM!" I rushed over to the section of the aisle that he'd been previously assigned.

There they were. A bright light seemed to shine around them and I could swear to this day that I heard angelic music playing in the background as I glanced at the treasure he'd discovered! Popsicles! Colors … flavors … fruit … sugar … sugar free … popsicles with riddle sticks, popsicles with stripes, it was a popsicle wonderland! The Disney World of frozen confection! We began selecting boxes and proclaiming statements like, "I think he'll like these!" "Oh, look at this!" and the ever popular, "I didn't know they made **these!"** And we didn't stop at popsicles, oh no! As the obsession grew, we moved on to bigger things: Italian ice cups, push-up bars, Creamsicles!

As we filled the cart with every conceivable combination of frozen ice and tropical fruit flavors, it was then I think we finally glanced at each other and realized we may have stepped over the line. We paused, glanced down at the cart and began a slow and almost inaudible giggle. The giggle soon mushroomed into a belly laugh so deep we had to bend forward and hold our stomachs. A release. In the midst of the most tragic, most morbid days of our lives, we laughed. We laughed until we cried. We cried until we laughed again.

As I look back and recall the Popsicle Caper of 2004, I realize, though pop did enjoy every popsicle we brought him that day, they did so much more for my brother and I than they did for him.

A Simple Truth About ...

Fun

I've learned that life is like a carnival
with all its sights and sounds;
sometimes you need to skip the rides
and just hang out with the clowns!

While the work or play is on, it is a lot of fun
if while you are doing one you don't
constantly feel that you ought to be
doing the other.

Life is not a journey to the grave with the
intention of arriving safely in a pretty and
well-preserved body, but rather
to skid in sideways, thoroughly used up,
totally worn out, and loudly proclaiming
"Wow! What a ride!"

Peter Sage

Today was good.

Today was fun.

Tomorrow is another one.

THEODOR GEISEL (DR. SEUSS)

I never lose sight of the fact

that just being is fun.

KATHARINE HEPBURN

Life is a great big canvas,

and you should throw all the

paint on it you can.

DANNY KAYE

A Simple Truth About ...

Success

I've learned that success should not be measured
in what you will buy or own,
but in the pride you feel
in the person you're with ...
when you are all alone.

Success

Recently I received an invitation to write a "how-to" article regarding the success of my small company, and I began by reflecting on the many different avenues and routes I'd taken, which ultimately led me toward my own "Road to Success."

Initially, I'd experienced a mental dilemma that involved the definition of the word "success." My dictionary read as follows: the achievement of something planned or attempted. Yet, my current success was neither planned nor attempted. It was more recognized and cultivated.

Recognized because I perceived and capitalized upon, an opportunity that required me to venture into a world completely out of the realm of my training and experience. Cultivated because I believed in it enough to devote my time, energy, and most importantly, my heart, to its development, growth and success.

Most columnists doling out advice on success would undoubtedly mention how important it is to set goals and have a strategy to help you achieve and accomplish each. I, too, feel it is important to set goals, yet I feel it is equally as important to remain flexible and fully aware of opportunities that arise during life's journey that may not follow suit with rigid plans and goals.

I spent more than twenty years in the corporate environment, seeking acknowledgement for my hard work and dedication, hoping to move up the corporate ladder. I had always written creatively as a hobby and began sending my work to a syndicated radio show in town. Before I knew it, opportunity was knocking at my door and I opened it as wide as I could. By following my passion, instead of the plans and goals I'd set, I discovered my own success.

There is a quote by Norman Vincent Peale that reads: "Throw your heart over the fence and the rest will follow." If I had to summarize this chapter into one sentence, that would have to be it. True success, complete success, is attained when you find personal fulfillment in what you do, instead of going through the motions of receiving a paycheck. **It comes down to making a life vs. making a living.**

As an inspirational author and poet, I've often had to walk a fine line between becoming a profitable business owner and owning up to the words I've written in my poems and stories. Though my first book and its products have now exceeded sales of more than a quarter of a million, and countless people from around the globe have read my work through the Internet, I truly believe that my legacy of success will be found more in the lives and hearts that have been touched by my words rather than in the balance in my bank account.

A Simple Truth About ...

Change

I've learned to become adaptable
to the coming of each season
for every leaf that changes color,
changes for a reason.

What the caterpillar calls the end of the world,
the master calls a butterfly.

RICHARD BACH

The truth is that our finest moments are most likely
to occur when we are feeling deeply
uncomfortable, unhappy, or unfulfilled.
For it is only in such moments, propelled by
our discomfort, that we are likely to step out
of our ruts and start searching for
different ways or truer answers.

M. SCOTT PECK

It is not the strongest of the species that survives,
nor the most intelligent, but the one
most responsive to change.

CHARLES DARWIN

The most successful people are those
who are good at plan B.

JAMES YORKE

View change as the one constant in your life.
Welcome it. Expect it. Anticipate it.

DENIS WAITLEY

Expectations

I've learned that to rely on "what might be" often results in a serious blunder.

Do not heat up the frying pan just because your bobber went under!

I would not anticipate the relish of any happiness,
nor feel the weight of any misery,
before it actually arrives.

Unknown

We simply assume that the way we see things
is the way they really are or the way they should be.
And our attitudes and behaviors grow
out of these assumptions.

Stephen R. Covey

Everything comes if a man will only wait.

Benjamin Disraeli

I know not any thing more pleasant, or more
instructive, than to compare experience with
expectation, or to register from time to time the
difference between idea and reality.
It is by this kind of observation that we grow
daily less liable to be disappointed.

Samuel Johnson

The sudden disappointment of a hope leaves a scar
which the ultimate fulfillment of that hope
never entirely removes.

Thomas Hardy

Forgiveness

I've learned the value of making amends
and how to bury my anger and sorrow,
for I wouldn't want them part of my legacy
should I never see a tomorrow.

Final Words

In stories I have previously penned, I have referenced one of my father's favorite sayings. He used to say in a joking manner, "I think we should all be born with expiration dates stamped on our foreheads … like a carton of milk." And since his death several years ago, I have often contemplated this unique concept, its simplicity and the obvious truth behind his rationalization. He was suggesting that if we somehow knew when and where we were destined to leave not one more footprint on this earth, it would somehow better the days we live on it.

It makes me wonder. If we did know when our "expiration date" was, how would that information lead us to do things differently? How would that knowledge affect the way we live our lives and treat others? Would we live consistently respecting others and showing our loved ones how much we care? Or would we live selfishly, insensitive to the feelings and needs of others, waiting until the closing days or hours to make amends, knowing that our "final words" are what would be considered most significant and therefore, most memorable?

I recently read an article about someone who attended a luncheon with several highly accomplished people. The speaker gave them two minutes to write a response to one question:

"If you knew you were dying, what would your final words be?"

Apparently, despite the highly polished resumes of those in attendance, not one of them referenced their notable accomplishments or spoke of their high-value material acquisitions. Instead, each attendee indicated their last words would be focused on their loved ones. That, in itself, speaks volumes regarding what should truly be considered "success" in life. Work, becoming successful and setting personal and professional goals to achieve, are all vitally important aspects of life. However, in the end, our true worth and significance comes not from what we have accomplished or attained, but in the legacy we have left in the hearts and minds of those we've loved and those who have loved us. When all is said and done, what will matter most are those relationships and bonds we've created with the people in our lives with whom we've shared love, laughter and memories.

Death is not known to be an efficient entity. Therefore, the date of our ultimate departure is not likely to be something we can prepare for in advance, or schedule on our busy calendar. There will be no notification email sent out with the subject: PENDING DEMISE. For most of us, it is highly unlikely that we will know our "expiration date" and therefore, be given the opportunity to speak heartfelt and articulately selected, "final words." The thought of that type of premeditation is uncomfortably morbid and truthfully, rather depressing for most of us.

However, after contemplating my own response to the speaker's question, it occurred to me, the days I am living now ARE my final words; not just the "words," but everything I am currently doing and saying to, or for, others. These are the things that will be remembered by my friends and loved ones. The way in which I am living my life, my actions, my relationships with them on a regular, everyday basis ARE my final words, which epitomizes the old adage, **"Actions speak louder than words."**

A Simple Truth About ...

Defenses

I've learned we shouldn't put up defenses,
even when we've gotten hurt;
instead of being more afraid,
we should just be more alert!

Sometimes you put walls up not to keep people out,
but to see who cares enough to break them down.

UNKNOWN

If you are carrying strong feelings about something
that happened in your past, they may hinder
your ability to live in the present.

LES BROWN

It is not reason but feeling which leads man
to the height of his destiny.

ALEXIS CARREL

Never apologize for showing feelings.
Remember that when you do,
you apologize for the truth.

BENJAMIN DISRAELI

Nobody can hurt me without my permission.

GANDHI

You cannot make yourself feel something
you do not feel, but you can make yourself
do right in spite of your feelings.

PEARL S. BUCK

A Simple Truth About ...

Sadness

I've learned no matter how deep your pain,
your sadness ... your yearning,

the sun will keep on rising

and the world will keep on turning.

When the clouds of sorrow gather over us
we see nothing beyond them,
nor can imagine how they will be dispelled;
yet a new day succeeds the night,
and sorrow is never long
without a dawn of ease.

SAMUEL JOHNSON

You cannot prevent the birds of sadness
from passing over your head, but you can prevent
their making a nest in your hair.

CHINESE PROVERB

There are as many nights as days,
and the one is just as long as the other
in the year's course.
Even a happy life cannot be without a measure
of darkness, and the word "happy" would
lose its meaning if it were not
balanced by sadness.

CARL JUNG

We enjoy warmth because we have been cold.

We appreciate light because we have been in

darkness. By the same token, we can experience

joy because we have known sadness.

DAVID WEATHERFORD

A Simple Truth About ...

Regret

I've learned that to experience each stage in life,
you must move on to the next place,
because you'll never score a home run
if you don't leave second base.

Your Own Friend

After sadly attending funeral services of friends and relatives, some leaving this earth long before "their time" was done, I have come to the realization that it is imperative that one become their own friend. I had sadly learned of the death of two women in particular; one a friend, one a cousin, who were both my age. I wondered as I grieved beside friends and family if each had even been granted enough time to become their own friend. I thought about this because often this realization doesn't hit us until we are past the summer season of our youth and well into the fall or winter of our lives. I've recently begun trying to befriend myself. I know this may sound strange to some, but it's true. I am no longer being so hard on myself and not nearly as critical. As I've grown older, I've realized that much of what I have wasted precious minutes fretting over, does not *truly* matter and never will.

In my first book, I wrote about a letter that was received and routed around my office many years ago. It was written by the wife of an employee who knew she hadn't much time to live. This letter made such an impact on my life that I saved a copy of it and continue to live by these words she'd written:

"Regrets? I have a few. Too much worrying. I worried about finding the right husband and having children, being on time, being late and so on. It didn't matter. It all works out and it would have worked out without the worry and the tears. If I would have known then what I know now. But, I did and so do you. We're all going to die. Stop worrying and start loving and living."

Stop worrying and start living. Words to live by.

Armed with a cheap calculator, (I did not inherit a math gene) I recently computed that I spend three hours per month, which equates to an approximate 36 hours per year … folding towels! That's a day-and-a-half out of my life every year turning absorbent terrycloth rectangles into absorbent terrycloth squares! I won't even do the math on fitted sheets! Why? Because somebody somewhere made the unwritten "rule" that this is the way things must be done, and generations of mothers have passed this important skill onto their sons and daughters as one of the crucial items on the "right" way to do things list.

Just for one CRAZY moment, think what would happen if you didn't spend those hours folding towels, and just haphazardly wadded them up right out of the dryer and put them on a shelf in your linen closet! Oh the horror! However, would they be any less clean? Would they be any less hard to reach? No. This is one of the needless things I am referring to that I have given far too much time and effort towards. Yet, I will continue to fold my perfect squares and stack them neatly on a shelf because it is ingrained in me.

It makes me wonder about the other meaningless items that society has programmed into my head. For instance, has anyone ever been denied access through the gates of Heaven because he used his salad fork to eat his potatoes? Has anyone ever seen etched upon a tombstone … "Mrs. Smith is buried here in the clay … (Pssst … she wore *white* shoes *after* Labor Day!)" Has anyone lead an unfulfilled life because they never learned how to properly fold a fitted sheet?

The answer is no. I have a long list of things I used to worry and fret over until I realized they do not matter in the scheme of life. If you do choose to worry, worry about what does.

Or, in the concise, experienced words of my teenage niece, learn to just "chillax," (apparently a combination of "chill out" and "relax"). Don't sweat the small stuff or be too critical of yourself. Learn to be your own friend. Everyone has his or her own time here … this time is YOURS. Don't spend it filled with fret and regret.

A Simple Truth About ...

Blame

I've learned that it is always best
to accept responsibility;
to "fess up when you mess up"
is the best philosophy.

It is always easier to confess the sins of others
than to acknowledge our own faults,
and to point out the delinquencies of others
than to mend our own nets.

J.B. CHAPMAN

Every man is his own captain on the voyage of life;
if shipwrecked, he alone is to blame.

ELLA E. DODSON

If something goes wrong, it is more important
to talk about who is going to fix it
than who is to blame.

FRANCIS J. GABLE

Most people would learn from their mistakes
if they weren't so busy trying to place
the blame on someone else.

Vern McLellan

A man should never be ashamed
to own he has been wrong, which is but saying,
in other words, that he is wiser today
than he was yesterday.

Alexander Pope

Your life is the fruit of your own doing.
You have no one to blame but yourself.

Joseph Campbell

A Simple Truth About ...

Simplicity

I've learned the phrase, "less is more"
is absolutely true ...
with too much of what you don't need,
it's hard to find the things you do!

Everything we possess that is not necessary
for life or happiness becomes a burden,
and scarcely a day passes that
we do not add to it.

ROBERT BRAULT

Simplicity is making the journey of this life
with just baggage enough.

AUTHOR UNKNOWN

The wisdom of life consists in the
elimination of non-essentials.

LIN YUTANG

Have nothing in your house
that you do not know to be useful
or believe to be beautiful.

WILLIAM MORRIS

Out of clutter, find simplicity.
From discord, find harmony.
In the middle of difficulty
lies opportunity.

ALBERT EINSTEIN

Worry

I've learned there's truth in what I've heard:
"fretting what may never come true
is like paying interest on a loan
before it ever becomes due."

Partly Cloudy

Recently, I was checking the weekly weather outlook to help me decide when and where to take a spur-of-the-moment road trip. I noticed the particular wording that the forecasters used in their "guesstimation" of the amount of sunshine we'd be offered the following week versus the amount of clouds. The two words that I read were: "Partly Cloudy." I started thinking about the phrase they'd chosen to describe the weather and repeated it aloud: "Partly cloudy … Partly cloudy."

I started thinking, if part of the day is to be considered cloudy, of what must the other part of the day consist? The word SUNNY is the only thing that came to my mind! So why did they use the phrase partly cloudy instead of partly sunny? Is it because there is some scientific formula that calculates the precise atmospheric conditions that tip the weather scales to change a "partly sunny" forecast into a "partly cloudy" one?

Is it because the weather person wants us to be pleasantly surprised when we begin to feel the sun's warm rays upon our skin? Or could it be because they view the world with a glass half-empty attitude?

Say for the sake of argument that a "partly cloudy" forecast could also be defined as "mostly sunny." That would mean that a "mostly cloudy" forecast could mean a "partly sunny" day. Now, doesn't that sound more like a prediction around which you'd like to plan your day's events?

My new positive outlook theory led me to evaluate my own attitude. I have to admit that I have a tendency to initially view life's situations with a "partly cloudy" frame of mind, often focusing on the negative instead of the positive.

But when I looked back at the weather forecast hoping for more insights into life, I was disappointed again when I saw that the forecaster took yet another turn onto Pessimistic Avenue. I read the words, "30% chance of precipitation." Why not go with the odds here? Would they be stepping out too far on the weather prediction limb to report a 70% chance of clear skies instead?

It all comes down to a personal choice. If I choose to focus on the 30% precipitation in my life, instead of the 70% sunshine, I will continually be anticipating dark clouds that may never appear. It is those things that may or may not ever happen, that lead to a negative, "partly cloudy" attitude. I have discovered that happiness is more easily found if you choose to believe that a *mostly cloudy* forecast really means a *partly sunny* day!

A Simple Truth About ...

Failure

I've learned that every loss or defeat
reveals an important surprise ...
for time will prove each setback,
was a blessing in disguise.

Failure should be our teacher, not our undertaker.
Failure is delay, not defeat.
It is a temporary detour,
not a dead-end street.

DENIS WAITLEY

Once you've failed, analyze the problem and
find out why, because each failure is one more step
leading up to the cathedral of success.

CHARLES F. KETTERING

Failure is success if we learn from it.

MALCOLM FORBES

If you see failure
as a monster stalking you,
or one that has already ruined your life,
take another look.
That monster can become a benevolent teacher,
opening your mind to successes
you cannot now imagine.

MARTHA BECK

What is defeat? Nothing but education;

nothing but the first step to something better.

WENDELL PHILLIPS

A Simple Truth About ...

Procrastination

I've learned the negative effects
of being the worst procrastinator,
but I can't seem to help myself,
so I will write about that ... later.

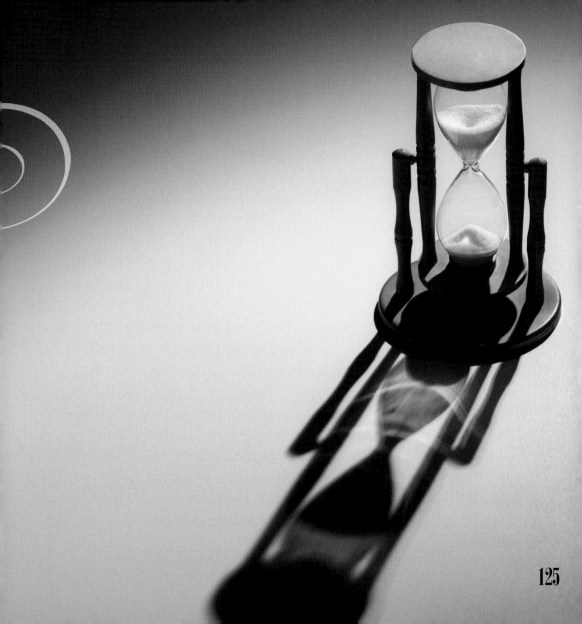

125

TUIT

My father had a special way of making his point. I'm learning every day that those unique ways he had to ensure his lessons were imprinted in my mind, actually worked.

One of the most vivid examples of my father's unique style of parenting was his response to my lack of enthusiasm when he had requested that I take care of something. I distinctly remember having a habit of answering my dad's requests to do chores with, "When I get around to it ..." This answer was not the response my father preferred from any of his children, but unfortunately the one he received most often, at least from me.

One particular afternoon my father politely requested that I complete some mundane chore that apparently I didn't find particularly interesting. I answered him curtly with my standard, "I'll do it, dad. When I get around to it!" I couldn't help but notice the unmistakable *cat that ate the canary grin* on his face as he reached into his pocket and handed me a little cardboard circle, about two inches in diameter. Both sides were printed with nothing but the word, "TUIT."

Yes, he had, in essence, found a way of making sure that I'd gotten a round tuit. At the time, I remember trying to appear as unimpressed as possible because the result of this little gag was my having to do whatever task had been requested of me that day.

Now, many years later, I find myself applying this round tuit philosophy to the daily struggle of prioritizing my endless list of "to dos." As I push those less important tasks to the bottom of the list, such as: "visit Aunt Margaret" or "call mom" or "make lunch plans with Susan," I can almost hear myself saying "I'll do it when I get around to it."

Well, not anymore. Recently I placed a round tuit on the top of my to do list. Those items listed under it have become #1 priority and the others will just have to wait their turn. Life is too short, and putting off doing meaningful things because other tasks get in the way is no excuse anymore.

In the back of your mind, you probably have some of those things that are easily put off, yet most important.

Maybe it's time to analyze your priorities and find out what's stopping you from getting a round tuit.

A Simple Truth About ...

Life

I've learned there are certain things
that may never be fully understood
for life isn't always fair ...
but it's still pretty darn good!

I like living. I have sometimes been wildly, despairingly, acutely miserable, racked with sorrow, but through it all I still know quite certainly that just to be alive is a grand thing.

AGATHA CHRISTIE

The only question in life is whether or not you are going to answer a hearty 'Yes!' to your adventure.

JOSEPH CAMPBELL

There are two ways to live your life. One is as though nothing is a miracle. The other is as though everything is a miracle.

ALBERT EINSTEIN

When you arise in the morning,
think of what a precious privilege it is to be alive –
to breathe, to think, to enjoy, to love.

MARCUS AURELIUS

Life is what we make it;
always has been,
always will be.

ANNA MARY ROBERTSON (GRANDMA MOSES)

A Simple Truth About ...

Time

I've learned that watches and clocks
may someday stand still ...
but the time that they measure?
It never will!

960 Minutes.

According to my calculations and my current schedule, that's how many minutes, approximately, averaged, that I spend awake out of the 1,440 minutes contained within each "day." Therefore, I strongly consider each of them to be MY minutes and they belong to no one but me. I, alone, have the choice where and with whom I choose to share my minutes and what situations or emotions are (or aren't) worthy of utilizing these precious commodities.

When applicable, I find myself repeating the phrase: "Choose how you use." Just as you ask yourself before making a purchase, "Is this really worth my money?" ask yourself before engaging in negativity or cynicism, "Is this really worth my minutes?" Before you start worrying about something that may never materialize, ask yourself, "Is it worth my minutes?"

Today, we watch how we would spend 960 dollars more carefully than how we would spend the same amount of minutes, our daily ration of time, though the latter is far more precious to behold and should be budgeted with the utmost attention to detail. Instead, often we'll spend our 960 minutes as though they were recyclable or in endless supply.

When you lay your head down tonight and preview in your mind how you spent your allotted 960 minutes, which words will best describe the answer? Did you share your minutes with contentment, laughter and joy or did you choose to share too much of this finite resource today with anger, resentfulness and aggravation?

A good example of my new thought process was played out the other day in the parking lot of my local grocery store. A woman (dialing her cell phone) ignored a stop sign and pulled directly in front of my car. With a dexterity that would have made Mario Andretti envious, I swerved and somehow missed hitting her SUV. Afterwards, however, when she should have chosen to express gratitude, I turned and noticed her hand gestures, which unmistakably and vehemently expressed sentiments quite the opposite. My blood pressure rose rapidly, but through gritted teeth, I repeated to myself silently, "Choose how you use … choose how you use."

I chose to continue to drive forward, unresponsive to her provocational actions. I'm not going to fib and say I didn't spend five or ten minutes in anger or distress over the incident because I certainly did. However, I then let it go. I let it go. I did not let it fester and eat up more minutes than it should have. The situation simply wasn't worthy of using up my minutes. In fact, writing these two paragraphs is the first time I've recalled the incident since. I remember thinking that evening, as a strategy for my new 960 minutes theory, that maybe I should stay awake ten minutes later just to recoup the lost time!

I say use your minutes wisely; don't let others dictate how you spend them. This is not to say you should quit your job today, but just **remember that your minutes are completely non-refundable; you can't buy more,** you can't borrow someone else's and you can't get them back once they're gone.

If only the rules stated that when we reached 90 years of age, we could simply write a letter to the "Life Customer Service Department" stating, "In 2008, I spent 10,950 minutes filled with aggravation and frustration. Since the customer is always right, I am officially requesting that those misspent minutes be added back to my life's account. I will await your confirmation. Thank you."

I've often thought about the cell-phone company commercials where they say their calling plan is better than their competitor's plan because their minutes "roll over." Wouldn't it be wonderful if life worked that way; if we could only use the minutes of the day we'd like and let the others roll over into the next day, week or month? But we all know that life's "calling plan" doesn't offer rollover minutes and our only option is to use them or lose them.

Life has its moments and unfortunately, there are times when sadness and despair are inescapable. However, 30 minutes per day spent in avoidable discontent equates to more than one week per year from your life; seven days, which could have instead been lived ...enjoyed ... relished and celebrated. *It's your choice.*

The longer I live, the more I realize that everything in life, no matter how insignificant it may seem, has a reason and a purpose. Everything we see, do, hear and learn eventually plays a part in our journey. In time, we learn that disappointments are but inevitable blessings and that no matter how difficult the situation may seem, or how much worrying we invest, we will make it through. If we were all born with these Simple Truths inherent, then life's lessons would have no reason or purpose as we'd have nothing to learn from them and nowhere to grow. Life is a teacher … and a classroom … and we are its students.

Every person we meet, whether they become lifelong friends or summer acquaintances, leaves us with something of value. I believe every crossed path has not crossed by happenstance and every emotion we experience, from grief to elation, or hatred to love, only helps us grow during and following the experience. Unfortunately, it is not until we grow older that we recognize and learn to appreciate life's lessons. I wrote this last Simple Truth to summarize that thought:

A Simple Truth about...

Awareness

I feel as though I'm a victim of crime;
as if time has committed a theft
for I didn't truly begin to appreciate life
until I had less of it left!

I compare life to an infinite-piece jigsaw puzzle. We start with a clear table, upon which we add countless colors, designs and shapes. It is up to us to accept and examine them one by one and figure out just where they fit. Every person we meet, every lesson we learn, gives us yet another piece to help us solve our puzzle. The more pieces we acquire, the clearer the whole picture becomes.

And as our "puzzle" grows, so do we. We change as we learn these Simple Truths and simultaneously, subconsciously and consistently gather more pieces. We evolve and adapt. The way in which we react to certain situations is a direct result of how we've reacted to similar situations we've experienced. The decisions we make today are because of those decisions — both good and bad — that we've made previously. The way in which we treat the people in our lives today is a reflection of how we've treated, and how we've been treated by, others in our past. We learn to worry less and appreciate more. We learn that it brings us joy if we stop and listen to the sound of a child's laughter. We learn how to say, "I'm sorry" without hesitation. Most importantly, we learn that life is not forever. In other words, our past alters our future. The Simple Truths of yesterday pave the way and open our minds to readily accept, and learn from, those we'll encounter tomorrow.

In closing, I hope you've enjoyed reading some of my "puzzle pieces" in this book. Maybe you'll find that they will add an important piece or two, as you continue to collect and connect the pieces of your own puzzle.

Linda Ellis

About the Author

Linda Ellis started writing creatively as a child, a talent inherited from her Irish grandmother. She grew up in Florida and then moved to New York for several years. However, her southern roots kept calling her home and she settled in Georgia where she now lives with her family.

She spent many years working in the corporate environment, but after her first poem was shared on a syndicated radio program in 1994, an alternative career began to emerge and she soon came to the realization that her true passion was writing.

Because no promotion or raise received from her boss could ever equal the satisfaction she felt when she heard from those whose hearts had been touched by her words, she made the decision to leave the corporate world behind to pursue her dream: inspiring others through her writing and speaking.

Millions of people have been touched by her words and today she shares her inspirations through her company, "Linda's Lyrics." In addition to writing, she is an inspirational speaker and makes a special connection with her audiences through her insightful and thought-provoking presentations.

Simple Truths of Life follows the success of her gift book, *The Dash, Making a Difference with Your Life,* co-authored with Mac Anderson. Her next book, *Every Single Day,* is scheduled for publication in 2010.

For more information about Linda, visit: www.lindaellis.net

THE SIMPLE TRUTHS DIFFERENCE

If you have enjoyed this book we invite you to check out our entire collection of gift books, with free inspirational movies, at **www.simpletruths.com**.

You'll discover it's a great way to inspire *friends* and *family,* or to thank your best *customers* and *employees.*

Our products are *not available in bookstores ... only direct.* Therefore, when you purchase a gift from Simple Truths you're giving something that can't be found elsewhere!

For more information, please visit us at:
www.simpletruths.com

Or call us toll free...
800-900-3427